Contents

Any words appearing in the text in bold, **like this,** are explained in the glossary. You can also look out for them in the Word Bank box at the bottom of each page.

Where in the world?

St Patrick

St Patrick is the patron saint of Ireland. He came to the country in AD 432 to convert the Irish to Christianity. He famously used the three-leaved Irish **shamrock** to explain the Holy Trinity of the Father, the Son, and the Holy Spirit in the Christian tradition. Legend also has it that St Patrick chased all the snakes from Ireland – there are none today!

From your hotel room you can hear music and cheering in the streets outside. You decide to investigate, and as you step outside on to the street, you are swept along in a tide of people. Many of them are wearing green or carrying flags of green, white, and orange.

Suddenly you can see marching bands, and **floats** with dancers in brilliant costumes. There are street performers too. What is going on? Suddenly a voice behind you shouts out "Welcome to Dublin – and happy St Patrick's day". This gives you all the clues you need. Dublin is the capital of Ireland, and St Patrick is the country's **patron saint**. You are in Ireland, an island to the west of the United Kingdom, and the most westerly point in Europe.

Statues of St Patrick can be found all over Ireland.

WORD BANK   AD number of years from the birth of Jesus Christ in the Christian calendar
float decorated platform built on a vehicle used in carnivals

Destination Detectives

Ireland

North
America

Europe

Asia

IRELAND

Africa

South
America

Australasia

Rob Bowden and Ronan Foley

Raintree

www.raintreepublishers.co.uk
Visit our website to find out more information about **Raintree** books.

To order:
☎ Phone 44 (0) 1865 888112
▤ Send a fax to 44 (0) 1865 314091
▢ Visit the Raintree Bookshop at **www.raintreepublishers.co.uk** to browse our catalogue and order online.

Produced for Raintree by
White-Thomson Publishing Ltd,
Bridgewater Business Centre,
210 High Street, Lewes, BN7 2NH

First published in Great Britain by Raintree,
Halley Court, Jordan Hill, Oxford OX2 8EJ,
Part of Harcourt Education.
Raintree is a registered trademark of
Harcourt Education Ltd.

Editorial: Sonya Newland, Melanie Waldron,
and Lucy Beevor
Design: Gary Frost
Picture Research: Amy Sparks
Production: Chloe Bloom

Originated by Modern Age
Printed and bound in Hong Kong

Hardback:
10 digit ISBN 1406203114
13 digit ISBN 9781406203110
10 9 8 7 6 5 4 3 2 1
11 10 09 08 07 06

Paperback:
10 digit ISBN 140620322X
13 digit ISBN 9781406203226
10 9 8 7 6 5 4 3 2 1
12 11 10 09 08 07

British Library Cataloguing in Publication Data
Bowden, Rob
  Ireland. - (Destination detectives)
  1.Ireland - Geography - Juvenile literature 2.Ireland -
  Social life and customs - 21st century - Juvenile
  literature 3.Ireland - Civilization - Juvenile literature
  I.Title II.Foley, Ronan
  941.7'0824

Acknowledgements
Corbis pp. 8-9 (Barry Cronin/ZUMA), 13 (Rougemont
Maurice), 17 (Paul McErlane/Reuters), 18 (Gideon Mendel),
19 (Richard Cummins), 36 (David Turnley); Getty Images
pp. 26-27 (Lonely Planet Images); Photolibrary pp. 6t (Jon
Arnold Images), 6b (Index Stock Imagery), 23
(Images.Com), 25t (Jon Arnold Images), 25b, 26 (Nonstock
Inc.), 27 (Index Stock Imagery), 30-31 (Jon Arnold Images),
30, 32 (Index Stock Imagery), 33, 34-35 (Index Stock
Imagery), 42-43 (Photononstop); Topfoto pp. 4, 5, 10 (Keith
Jones), 11, 14, 16, 22 (Fastfoto Picture Library), 24
(Fastfoto Picture Library), 29 (John Balean), 31, 35 (Robert
Piwko), 37 (Spectrum Colour Library), 38 (John Balean), 39
(Fastfoto Picture Library), 40, 41, 43 (Fastfoto Picture
Library); WTPix pp. 5t, 5m, 5b, 12-13, 15, 20, 21, 28.

Cover photograph reproduced with permission of
Photolibrary.

Every effort has been made to contact copyright
holders of any material reproduced in this book.
Any omissions will be rectified in subsequent
printings if notice is given to the publishers.

The paper used to print this book comes from
sustainable resources.

You get back to watching the parade, along with the other 1.5 million people who come every year to enjoy the St Patrick's Festival in Dublin. It is an exciting introduction to this ancient country, which is known for its friendly people and beautiful landscapes.

People push a giant statue of St Patrick down O'Connell Street in Dublin during the St Patrick's Day parade.

Find out later...

What type of dancing is this?

Which river runs through Ireland's capital city?

How are the Irish protecting their fishing industry?

patron saint holy person who is the guardian of a place or people
shamrock small plant common across Ireland

The Emerald Isle

Back in your hotel, you see a map with notes displayed on the wall near the reception desk. The sign next to it says "Welcome to the Emerald Isle". The person at the desk tells you that Ireland is often called this because of its green landscape. The map gives you some clues about what to discover in Ireland.

Ireland at a glance

SIZE: 70,280 square kilometres (27,135 square miles)

OFFICIAL NAME: Republic of Ireland

POPULATION: 4 million

CAPITAL: Dublin

TYPE OF GOVERNMENT: Republic

OFFICIAL LANGUAGES: English and Irish

CURRENCY: Euro (€)

Ireland's west coast is well known for its rugged cliffs, **inlets**, and islands. It is popular with tourists and with the thousands of birds that nest on the cliffs.

The capital city, Dublin, is a mix of fascinating history, large parks and gardens, a busy **port**, and modern shops.

WORD BANK   Celts group of people who lived in Europe from 2,000–4,000 years ago
Gaelic anything relating to the **Celts**

Ireland is famous for its strong **Gaelic** culture. The music, dance, art, sport, and language of Gaelic Ireland are all worth finding out about.

The Irish spirit

One thing you will never be short of while exploring Ireland is someone to talk to. The Irish are said to be some of the friendliest people in the world. They enjoy socializing with one another, and make strangers feel instantly welcome.

Just south of Dublin lie the beautiful Wicklow Mountains. They are popular with walkers and cyclists, and are known for their wild and beautiful scenery.

Cork, on the south coast, is Ireland's second-largest city, and is built on an island in the River Lee. It is an historic port, with many reminders of its trading past.

inlet small bay along a coastline
port place where ships load and unload cargo

Ancient origins

Not far from Dublin is a reminder of Ireland's ancient past. At Brú na Bóinne ("Bend in the Boyne") in County Meath you can discover **archaeological** remains that are older than the great pyramids of Egypt. They include burial chambers built by some of the first people to live in Ireland, more than 5,000 years ago.

The Celts

Many different peoples have settled in Ireland over the centuries. The **Celts** came to Ireland from northern Britain in around 600 BC. It was the Celts who introduced forms of writing, language, and art that became Ireland's **Gaelic** culture of today. Vikings first came to Ireland from Scandinavia in around AD 795. They took control of coastal settlements like Dublin, Waterford, and Limerick, and set up trade links with northern Europe.

Ogham

Ogham is an early Celtic alphabet that is still found in some parts of Ireland today. It has 25 characters, each one named after a tree or other natural feature, such as a feather. Each character is written as a horizontal line (representing a tree trunk), with lines coming from it (these are the branches) in different patterns.

These Ogham characters are "earth", "pine", and "feather".

WORD BANK archaeology study of remains to help us understand about the past

Invaders from England

The English came to Ireland in 1272, when King Henry II ordered the reform of Ireland's churches, and they soon ruled large parts of the island. Eventually, however, the English married into Irish families, and England began to lose control of Ireland.

In the 16th century, the English regained control, but by this time a lot had changed. The English became Protestant Christians in the 16th century, but Irish people remained Catholic Christians. The English Government took a lot of the Irish people's land and life was very difficult for the native people. Catholics were badly treated – many lived like slaves. In all, Ireland was under the control of the English for 750 years.

Newgrange, in Country Meath, was constructed around 3200 BC. It is believed to have been built as a tomb, and contains some of the earliest known Celtic carvings.

Dark foreigners

The Vikings began the settlements that became Ireland's greatest cities, including Dublin. One of the earliest places they settled was the area of Dublin known as Baldoyle, or Baile Dubh Ghaill, which means "town of the dark foreigners".

The Easter Rising

To the north of the country is the border between Ireland and Northern Ireland, which is part of the United Kingdom. But why is there a border here?

In 1916, a group of Irishmen staged a **rebellion** against British rule in Ireland. They took control of parts of Dublin, including the General Post Office in O'Connell Street. Standing on the steps of the Post Office, they declared a new Irish **republic**. This did not last, however, and the British took control again after just five days.

The Great Famine

For centuries, potatoes were the main crop grown in Ireland to feed its people. Between 1845 and 1849, however, the potato harvests failed because of a disease that attacked the crops. A terrible famine followed, and around 1 million people are believed to have died. About the same number left Ireland and went to live in Europe or the United States.

Fast fact
There are nearly as many Irish people in New York City, United States, as there are in Dublin. Seventy million people worldwide claim to have Irish **ancestry**.

The General Post Office in O'Connell Street, Dublin, was the focus of the 1916 Easter Rising, when the Irish rebelled against British rule.

WORD BANK   ancestry people you are descended from
rebellion when a group of people try to overthrow a government or ruler

A divided land

The British defeated the Irish Republicans, but many Irish people still wanted an end to British rule. Other Irish people wanted to be part of the United Kingdom. There was a divide between people loyal to Britain (the Loyalists) and those who wanted to create an independent Ireland (the Nationalists). After a war with Britain, called the War of Independence, an agreement was reached in 1921 to divide the country. The 26 southern counties became the Irish Free State, and the six northern counties became Northern Ireland. Both were still under some British control.

Not everyone agreed to the division, but the two parts are still separated today. The Irish Free State became completely independent from Britain in 1937. It was called the Republic of Ireland – the name it still has today – in 1949. Northern Ireland is still part of the United Kingdom, although some people there still want it to be joined with the rest of Ireland.

National anthem

Ireland's national anthem is called "Amhrán na bhFiann" – "The Soldier's Song". The words were first published in the newspaper *Irish Freedom* in 1912, and the chorus was adopted as the official national anthem in 1926. It tells of how the Irish will fight for their freedom from foreign rule.

Leinster House in Dublin has been home to the Irish parliament since 1922.

republic form of government where the people rule a country

11

Life in the cities

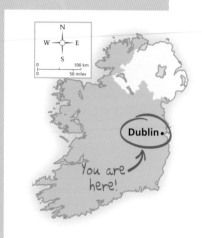

You are here!

You return to Dublin to discover more about living in Ireland's cities. Dublin is the capital city, and by far the largest in Ireland. There are over one million people living in Dublin and its **suburbs**. This is about 25 percent of the total population.

Dublin is the main business centre of Ireland, and is also home to the Irish Government. It has the best transport connections, with Ireland's main airport and two sea **ports**. The centre of Dublin is a popular shopping and entertainment area. Every year it attracts thousands of tourists from the United Kingdom, the United States, and Europe. It is now known as one of the great cities of Europe.

Immigrants

Many **immigrants** who come to live in Ireland from other countries end up in its cities, especially Dublin. Large numbers of Chinese, Russian, and Polish people live here. As these people settle in Ireland, they bring their cultures with them. Dublin, for example, now has Chinese supermarkets and Russian shops.

The River Liffey runs from the Wicklow Mountains, through the city of Dublin, and into Dublin Bay.

immigrants people who move from their own country and settle in another

Rich and poor

The River Liffey flows right through the middle of Dublin, splitting the city into the north side and the south side. The river also divides Dublin into richer and poorer areas. The south side is generally richer, with grand houses and wealthy neighbourhoods. The north side is poorer, with some low-quality housing. It also has higher levels of unemployment.

Temple Bar lies on the south side of the River Liffey. With its narrow, cobbled streets, shops, and restaurants, this is a popular area with tourists.

Temple Bar

Temple Bar was once a run-down part of Dublin south of the River Liffey. Today, it is an area filled with restaurants, art galleries, cinemas, theatres, and shops. It is also the centre of nightlife in Dublin, and has the most popular bars and clubs. It is a good example of how much Ireland has changed in the last twenty years.

suburbs areas of housing on the outskirts of a city or town

Ireland's main cities

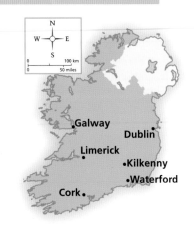

Ireland's second-largest city, Cork, is built on an island in the River Lee. It is well known for its festivals, including a film festival in October, and the International Jazz Festival. It is also an important **port**.

The largest city in the west of Ireland, Galway is known for its strong Irish and **Gaelic** traditions. It is a centre for music and poetry, theatre and dance. It also has a long history as a centre for fishing.

Ireland's smallest city

Kilkenny has just 8,600 people, and this makes it Ireland's smallest city. Although it is small, Kilkenny was once home to the Irish parliament. Today, the city is famous for its castle and for its arts and comedy festivals, which attract thousands of visitors every year.

Capital of Culture

In 2005, Cork was voted European Capital of Culture. This is a city selected every year by the **European Union** (EU), to help other countries understand the national culture and traditions of the chosen city.

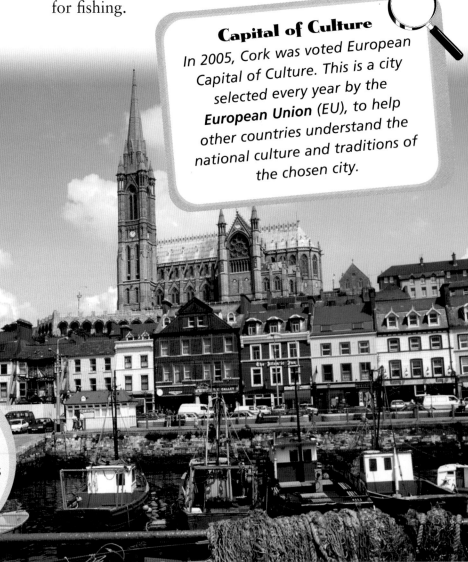

Cork Cathedral dominates the skyline of Ireland's second-largest city.

WORD BANK European Union group of countries that help each other with trade
hurling sport in which a leather ball is passed between players using sticks

An industrial town in the west of Ireland, Limerick is now being slowly redeveloped. It has important hi-tech industries in electronics, such as Dell Computers. Limerick is also known for its sport, and horseracing, rugby, Gaelic football, and **hurling** are all very popular here.

Waterford is the main commercial centre of south-east Ireland. It has been an important port since Viking times. Behind the port, the lively city centre is made up of a maze of narrow streets that are fun to explore.

Streets of water

Many of the main streets in Cork were once waterways in this busy historic port. As road transport took over from shipping, the waterways were filled in. St Patrick's Street, for example, once had **quays** for grand sailing ships. Along Grand Parade, the mooring posts from when ships moored here in the 18th century can still be seen.

Small boats moored on a river running through Waterford.

quay platform along the edge of a port or harbour for boats to load

Improving city life

In the north of Dublin, a new town called Ballymun is being built. It is situated on the old Ballymun housing estate, an area of high-rise flats that was built in the 1960s. The old flats were poorly built, and the estate had many problems of crime, unemployment, and poverty.

In 1997, Dublin City Council announced a plan to **regenerate** Ballymun. The old flats are being pulled down and a new town with housing, shops, and businesses is being built. When finished, it will be home to 30,000 people.

Blanchardstown

Blanchardstown opened in 1996. It is one of the largest purpose-built shopping centres in Europe. It was built on the edge of Dublin, close to the main motorway that goes around the city. It has over 10 million visitors each year, who spend an incredible one billion euros!

Ireland's Minister for Housing and Urban Renewal, Noel Ahern, starts the demolition of some of Dublin's old houses.

New housing is one of the most important parts of the plan, but Ballymun will also have a new high street to form a centre for the community. This will provide it with shops and other facilities. Community centres, sports halls, and open spaces are also part of the new plans.

City transport

Transport is another important part of the Ballymun plans. New bus links will improve connections between Ballymun and the city centre. They will also link it to the airport and nearby industrial regions. Both of these provide many job opportunities. There are also plans to link Ballymun to central Dublin by the new Luas light rail (**tram**) system.

The new Luas tram makes its way through the streets of Dublin.

Luas

A new city tram service called Luas (Irish for 'speed') began operating in June 2004. Each tram can carry 235–358 people. In total over a million people per month use Luas trams. The Luas trams can reach speeds of 70 kilometres (44 miles) per hour.

tram type of train that runs on rails through city streets

The booming economy

Projects like the **regeneration** of Ballymun are possible because Ireland's **economy** is "booming" – growing very strongly. This means there is a lot of money to invest in improving the country.

Ireland is a very good location for businesses because of its good transport links to Europe and the United States. It also has a skilful workforce and low business **taxes**. These attract international companies to Ireland. One of Ireland's most important industries is the information and communications technology (ICT) industry.

World leader

Ireland has become a world leader in computers and software. One-third of all the computers sold in Europe are made in Ireland. Apple, Dell, and IBM are some of the big companies with factories in Ireland. Ireland is also the world's biggest exporter of computer software. Microsoft has its European headquarters in Dublin.

Computers are made at the Dell factory in Limerick.

WORD BANK economy how a country makes and manages its money
export selling goods to another country

ICT

There are over 1,300 ICT companies in Ireland, and more than 91,000 ICT jobs. The ICT industry makes up 34 percent of all Ireland's **exports** – worth more than 30 billion euros a year. Most ICT companies are based in or around Dublin. Intel, for example, makes **microchips** at an enormous factory in Leixlip, on the outskirts of Dublin. It employs over 5,000 people and is Intel's largest factory outside the United States.

Other parts of the Irish economy, such as retail, leisure, construction and property, are all booming too. Many Irish people who once lived abroad are returning home to enjoy the benefits of Ireland's strong economy.

Ennis has become a model for e-towns across Ireland – and even the world.

E-town

In 1997, Ennis in County Clare became the world's largest information-age community. This meant that its homes, businesses, and schools were all connected to the latest computer technology. They used this technology to sell things and to communicate and share information electronically.

microchip part of a computer where all the information is decoded
taxes money collected by a government from income or sales

19

Culture & food

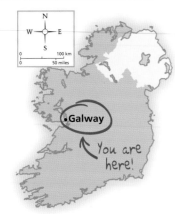

You are here!

From the buzz of modern Dublin, you head across Ireland to Galway to discover more about Ireland's traditions. Galway is at the heart of Ireland's culture, and it is here that you are most likely to still hear the Irish language spoken. There are many things to discover in Galway.

Irish dancing

Irish dancing dates back hundreds of years. It normally involves a group dance with fast-paced footwork to lively Irish music known as a reel or jig. An evening of Irish dancing is known as a céili. Céilis are held across Ireland and help to keep the tradition strong. Many people enjoy Irish dancing just for fun, but there are serious competitions too. The World Championships are held in Ireland, and bring together dancers from around the world.

The Gaeltacht

The Gaeltacht is the area of Ireland where Irish is still the main language. Galway is the gateway to the Gaeltacht region, which includes large parts of counties Donegal, Mayo, Galway, and Kerry (all on the west coast). It also includes parts of counties Cork, Meath, and Waterford. In total, there are around 86,000 people living in these Gaeltacht communities.

The Irish language

Irish is not widely spoken in Ireland today, but in the west of Ireland you may hear some words of Irish. Here are some useful phrases:

Fáilte Romh – Welcome

Conas a tá tu – How are you?

Slán – Goodbye

Go raibh maith agat – Thank you

Although the Irish language is no longer common in many parts of Ireland, signs often still use both English and Irish.

Oyster festival

In 1954, a local hotel owner began a small festival to celebrate the opening of the first oysters of the season. The festival soon grew into the Galway International Oyster Festival – one of Europe's top festivals. Each year, over 10,000 people gather in Galway to celebrate this event. The highlight is a competition to open 30 oysters as quickly as possible. The record is 1 minute 31 seconds.

Children learn Irish dancing from a young age, and enter competitions like this, in which they wear traditional dress.

Irish music

Galway is also well-known for its music, but to discover Irish music at its best you head south to County Clare – "the singing county". Miltown Malbay and Doolin are two places in County Clare where you are sure to find plenty of traditional tunes.

Most Irish music is played in "sessions", when musicians gather in a bar during the evening to enjoy playing music together. There are also music festivals, known as Fleadh Cheoils, held across Ireland. The most important of the festivals is Fleadh Cheoil na hÉireann, which is held in August in a different town each year. Irish music uses many different instruments. These include guitars, harps, accordions, flutes, tin whistles, and fiddles.

Modern music

Ireland's strong musical traditions have created some of the world's leading modern rock and pop artists too. By far the best known is the band U2. They started as a local Dublin band and went on to become the biggest band in the world.

The Irish band U2 have sold over 100 million records and their world tours sell out within hours!

WORD BANK   bagpipe wind instrument in which air blown into a bag produces notes on a set of connected pipes

Unusual instruments

There are also some more unusual instruments. The Uilleann pipe is a type of **bagpipe** that is very difficult to play. It is said that it takes seven years to learn, seven years to practise, and seven years to play before becoming an expert!

The bodhrán is a drum a little bigger than a tambourine. It is played with a wooden stick or with the back of the hand. The bodhrán is a popular tourist **souvenir** for visitors to Ireland.

People gather in pubs and bars in the evenings and dance to traditional live music.

The craic!

When people are enjoying themselves, they describe it as having the "craic". This means having a good time (a "crack"). It is often used to describe evenings with food, music, and good company – as in the phrase *ceoil, caint, agus craic* ("music, talk, and the crack").

souvenir something you buy as a reminder of a holiday

Irish food

All types of foods are available in Ireland today, but traditional dishes are still popular. Potatoes form the basis of much of the traditional diet, along with other vegetables (cabbages, onions, leeks, carrots, and parsnips) and meat (especially beef and lamb). Around the coasts, seafood is also popular. The west coast is well known for its delicious crabs and oysters. You find an Irish restaurant for a chance to try some of the local dishes on their menu.

Irish cheese

Ireland is famous for its dairy produce, and has some unique local cheeses. Counties Tipperary and Cork in the south-west of Ireland produce the most cheeses. Some of the best known are Cashel Blue, Cooleeney, Gubbeen, Knockanore, and Ardrahan – but there are many others.

Because Ireland is an island, fresh fish is a popular dish in many parts of the country.

Favourite dishes

Local dishes include:

- Soda Bread: Bread made with baking soda instead of yeast to make it rise when baked.
- Colcannon: Cooked potatoes fried with onions and cabbage or leeks in butter.
- Irish Stew: Lamb or beef cooked slowly with onions, carrots, parsnips, turnips, and potatoes.
- Dublin Coddle: Pork sausages and bacon cooked in cider with onions, garlic, potatoes, carrots, and herbs.
- Barm Brack: A sweet yeast bread made with dried fruit and spices. Popular at Halloween.

GUINNESS FOR STRENGTH

Guinness has been brewed in Ireland since 1759. ▲

A bowl of steaming colcannon – potatoes with cabbage. ▼

Brewing

Brewing is an important business in Ireland. Whiskey and beer are both produced, but Ireland is most famous for its stout, especially Guinness. Guinness is now brewed in over 50 countries and sold in over 150, but the best is still made in Ireland. It is so popular that the Guinness factory in Dublin is a major tourist attraction.

The Irish countryside

Having tried some Irish food, it is time to discover where it all comes from. Farming is an important activity in the Irish countryside, and Irish produce is **exported** as well as used locally. An area known as the "Golden Vale" in south-west Ireland is the main farming region. This is a good place to find out more.

Ireland has a mild climate, which makes its landscapes very green and fertile.

A wheat field after the harvest. Wheat is one of the most common crops grown in Ireland.

The Irish climate

Ireland has a wet and mild **climate**, and rarely suffers extremes of rain or temperature. This makes it perfect for farming, and especially for growing grass to graze cows. Vegetables also grow well in the Irish climate, especially potatoes, carrots, parsnips, and other root vegetables.

climate typical weather conditions in an area

Dairy farming

Ireland is well known for its dairy farming. There are around 23,800 dairy farmers. Between them they produce 5.3 million tonnes (5.2 million tons) of milk every year. Nearly all of this (80 percent) is exported – with most going to the countries of the **European Union**. Ireland provides 4.5 percent of all the milk in the EU, even though it has only 1 percent of the EU population.

Irish beef

After milk, Irish beef is Ireland's main farming produce. Ireland has some of the best grazing land in the world and so its beef is highly prized. Around 95 percent of Irish beef is exported and this was worth over 1.4 billion euros in 2004. Most exports are to the United Kingdom, Europe, and Russia.

Ireland has more than 7 million cattle – compared to 4 million people!

Organic farming

The number of **organic** farms in Ireland grew by more than four times between 1993 and 2005. Organic farming uses methods that protect the environment and avoid the use of chemicals. There are over 1,000 organic farmers, but they farm less than 1 percent of Irish farmland. Most organic farming is of beef and lamb.

Fishing

You will have discovered by now that in Ireland you are never far from the sea. The Irish seas are important for fishing. To find out more, you head to County Donegal in the very north of the country.

Killybegs, in County Donegal, is one of the main fishing towns in Ireland. From here, boats fish as far away as the waters between Scotland and Norway. Fish from Killybegs is sold in Ireland and around the world – in coutries as distant as Egypt or Japan!

Fish farming

Fish farms use large underwater cages to feed fish until they are ready to harvest. Salmon, oysters, and mussels are the most common species farmed in Ireland. Ireland is one of the first countries to produce organically farmed fish at farms like Clare Island, located 6 kilometres (3.7 miles) off the coast of County Mayo.

Fishing in Ireland is carefully monitored by the Government. This allows the fish to breed and increase in numbers.

angler *person who enjoys the sport of angling (fishing)*

A family business

Most fishing boats are family owned and run. There are around 1,400 boats in the Irish fishing fleet. When the fish are brought to land they are cleaned, processed, and packed, before being transported to markets.

The most important fish caught in Ireland is the mackerel, but others include herring, haddock, hake, and whiting. Shellfish like crabs, lobster, and scallops are also important.

Ireland's fisheries are carefully managed by the Government. Each month, the Government tells the fishing fleet how much it can catch. If too many of a particular type of fish are being caught, the Government puts a stop to the fishing.

Fast fact
More than 15,000 people work in the fishing industry in Ireland.

Fishing for fun

Fishing for pleasure is very popular in Ireland. Its rivers and lakes even attract **anglers** from overseas, especially for trout and salmon fishing. Anglers use special hooks called flies because they are disguised to look like real flies. A special flicking movement makes the fly move across the water. This fools the fish into taking a bite!

An angler holds up his catch at the end of a day's fishing on the River Barrow in Ireland.

Out west

Dingle is a small town in the Dingle peninsula, on the west coast of Ireland. It is a fishing village, popular with tourists, and an important centre for the surrounding villages. Its location makes it the most westerly town in Europe. It is also well known for Fungi, a dolphin that has become very friendly with the people of the town.

Village life

After a taste of the ocean life, you head back inland to explore the villages and towns that dot the Irish countryside. About 40 percent of Ireland's population still live in the countryside. This is much higher than in other European countries. In France, for example, it is 24 percent, 12 percent in Germany, and just 11 percent in the United Kingdom.

The **rural** population is very spread out, and many villages are not much more than a cluster of houses. Some are built around much larger manor houses, where local landowners once lived. The houses around them would have been for the workers.

Ireland's countryside is dotted with small villages, many of which are made up of just a few houses and a church.

Fungi the dolphin lives off the coast of Dingle, and is a great tourist attraction!

Expanding villages

Other villages have grown bigger because of trade or because they are on an important transport route. They normally have some shops and rural services, such as a post office, school, or church. In some villages and small rural towns, buildings have several uses. In Abbeyleix, County Laois, for example, the local greengrocer's store doubles up as the town's pub. Pubs in other villages are combined with hardware shops, bakeries, butchers, and post offices.

The post office in the village of Carlingford, in County Louth.

Buying the village

The price of houses in Ireland's villages is rising very quickly. This is because wealthy people from the cities are buying village homes to escape the bustle of the city at weekends. Sometimes they rent them out to tourists. This is making housing too expensive for some people who live and work in the Irish countryside.

Nature & wildlife

There is not much of Ireland that has not been touched by humans. There are still some important natural **habitats**, though, including Ireland's peat **bogs**. Many of these bogs are found right in the centre of Ireland. The town of Tullamore in County Offaly is surrounded by peat bogs and is a good place to learn more.

Peat wildlife

Ireland's peat bogs are home to several rare species of plants and animals. Some of the plants, including types of sundew, butterwort, and bladderwort, have adapted so well to the environment that they cannot grow anywhere else.
The bogs are also important for types of birds like the dunlin, which go there to breed.

Peat bogs

Peat bogs are made up of the remains of rotting plants and animals. These sank to the bottom of shallow lakes that covered this part of Ireland around 10,000 years ago. Between 85 and 95 percent of a peat bog is made up of water. This means they are very spongy to walk on. Special paths called toghers were built to cross the bogs. These were made from wooden planks laid along wooden rails, a bit like a railway track. The best example of a togher is Corlea togher in County Longford. **Archaeologists** have dated this ancient bog path to 148 BC, which means that it is over 2,150 years old! Ireland's peat bogs are between 2 and 12 metres (6 and 40 feet) in thickness and they cover about one-sixth of the country.

Dried peat, or pressed peat briquettes, are sold as a fuel for heating homes.

WORD BANK   bogs areas of soft, marshy land
habitat place where animals or plants live, such as a forest or the ocean

Peat secrets

Peat bogs are excellent at **preserving** things, and have provided many interesting glimpses into Ireland's past. Coins, jewellery, shoes, and dug-out canoes have all been found! Most interesting of all, many bodies have been discovered in the bogs – over 80 in total. One found in 1821 at Callagh bog in County Galway is over 2,000 years old!

These men are cutting peat into blocks, which will be used as a fuel.

preserve stop from decaying or spoiling

Conservation

At least half of Ireland's original peat **bogs** have been cleared for fuel, farmland, **forestry**, or other uses. Only 19 percent of Ireland's original bogs are still in good condition. Efforts are now being made to protect Ireland's remaining bogs, along with other important natural **habitats**. Six national parks have been created in Ireland and are managed by the National Parks and Wildlife Service (NPWS). To discover more, you head to the Wicklow Mountains National Park. The park was set up in 1991 and is located just to the south of Dublin.

Glenveagh National Park
Co. Donegal

Ballycroy National Park
Co. Mayo

Connemara National Park
Co. Galway

The Burren National Park
Co. Clare

Killarney National Park
Co. Kerry

Wicklow Mountains National Park
Co. Wicklow

Ireland's national parks have been created to conserve the peat bogs and other natural habitats.

Turloughs

Turloughs are "dry lakes". These form in areas of **limestone** when heavy rainfall fills the rock spaces and comes to the surface. Turloughs are under threat in Ireland because of drainage to make way for farmland. Six of Ireland's rarest plants can be found in and around turloughs.

WORD BANK   forestry planting and caring for trees
granite hard grey rock formed by heat beneath Earth's surface

Mountains of Wicklow

The Wicklow Mountains are an area of low **granite** hills, woodland, and peat bogs. The area is home to most of Ireland's mammals, including deer, badgers, foxes, otters, hares, and red squirrels, and over 80 nesting bird species. Protecting these while still allowing people to enjoy the park is a great challenge. Marked pathways help to protect the most fragile areas, and there are strict rules about land use inside the park boundaries.

The Wicklow Mountains are very beautiful, and are one of the most visited parts of Ireland.

The Wicklow Way

The Wicklow Way was Ireland's first long-distance path, and was opened in 1980. It begins on the edge of Dublin, and runs south-west across the Wicklow Mountains to the village of Clonegal. It is 132 kilometres (82 miles) long, and it takes between five and eight days to walk the total length.

Signs like this indicate a path that is good for walking and hiking in Ireland's national parks.

limestone soft rock formed by the skeletons of small animals

Everyday life

After exploring the wilderness of Wicklow, you head to nearby Bray. This is a seaside town to the south of Dublin, and a typical Irish town. It is a good place to discover what daily life is like in Ireland. Where do people study? How do they get around? What do they do for fun?

Education

Ireland has a very good education system, and all children must go to school between the ages of six and sixteen. Most children start earlier and stay longer. Around 80 percent complete their secondary leaving certificate when they are seventeen or eighteen years old.

Gaelscoileanna

Gaelscoileanna are schools where students are taught in the Irish language instead of English. They were introduced at the beginning of the 20th century, to make sure that the Irish language was not forgotten. A primary gaelscoil is called a bunscoil and a secondary one is called a meanscoil.

Children attend primary school between the ages of four and twelve in Ireland.

The main stages of education in Ireland are:

- Primary school – all children attend primary school, beginning at the age of four in nursery (kindergarten) and continuing until they are twelve.
- Secondary school – this is divided into three stages. The junior stage lasts three years or until children are fourteen. They then take Junior Certificate Exams. Many students then take a Transition Year, where they can study new, different subjects and take up work experience. After this, they go back to school for another two years until they take Leaving Certificate Exams.
- Higher education – called "third level" in Ireland, this can be a college or university course. Ireland has seven universities and many colleges.

Trinity College

The oldest university in Ireland is Dublin University, also known as Trinity College. It first opened in 1592, and now has over 12,000 students. The library here is very famous, and holds more than 4.25 million books!

Students celebrate their graduation outside Trinity College in Dublin – the most famous university in Ireland.

Canals

Ireland has two major canals – the Grand Canal and the Royal Canal. They both run from Dublin across the peat **bogs** of middle Ireland to the River Shannon in the west. The Grand is 132 kilometres (82 miles) long, and the Royal 145 kilometres (90 miles) long. The canals were opened in the 18th century and were used for carrying cargo.

Transport

From Bray there are many transport options available for travelling to other parts of Ireland. The town is connected to Dublin via the DART (Dublin Area Rapid Transport) train system. This was opened in 1984 and was designed to carry 35,000 passengers in and out of Dublin every day. It was upgraded between 2003 and 2005, and now carries 90,000 passengers a day. You decide to take the DART back into Dublin to explore other options.

Ferries

The DART train to Dublin passes Dún Laoghaire, one of Ireland's main ferry **ports**, carrying passengers and goods across the Irish Sea to the United Kingdom. Dublin, Rosslare, and Cork also have ferry ports connecting Ireland to different parts of the United Kingdom and beyond.

Today, both the Grand Canal (pictured) and the Royal Canal are being restored, and are used for pleasure boating.

WORD BANK   congestion blocking of roads due to large numbers of vehicles

Bus, rail, and air

From Connolly station in the heart of Dublin, you leave the DART. Trains leave Connolly station to other parts of Ireland along a total rail network of 1,947 kilometres (1,210 miles). The other main station is Dublin Heuston, on the west side of the city. Just outside Connolly station is the main bus station. From here, Bus Éireann (Bus Ireland) and several other companies offer services across the country. There are also special buses to Dublin airport, the main international airport. Shannon airport is Ireland's other main airport.

Ireland's transport network showing main rail routes, airports, and ferry ports.

People crowd the platform at Dublin's Connolly Station.

Women's football

Women's **Gaelic** football is the fastest-growing sport in the country. It first grew in popularity in the 1970s. Originally people thought it was just a passing craze, but the Ladies Gaelic Football Association of Ireland was founded in 1974, and today teams from all over Ireland compete in the All-Ireland Championship.

Leisure and sport

For many people in Ireland, leisure time is spent with friends and family. Others enjoy visiting historical places or walking in the countryside. One thing that nearly everyone enjoys in Ireland, however, is sport. As you catch a train to Limerick, a major sporting city, a paper left on the train explains some popular Irish sports.

Gaelic football

Gaelic football is an Irish version of soccer. Players can use their hands or feet to dribble, punch, or kick the ball at their opponent's goal. A point is given if the ball goes between the goalposts but over the crossbar. Three points are given for scoring under the crossbar into a net. There are fifteen players on each side, and it is played across two 35-minute periods.

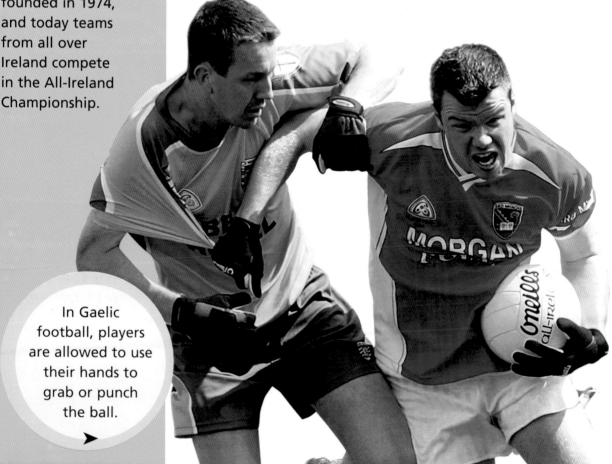

In Gaelic football, players are allowed to use their hands to grab or punch the ball.

Hurling

Hurling is a fast sport, in which a stick called a hurley is used to juggle and hit a ball over or under the opposing team's goal. Each team has fifteen players, and they pass the ball to each other, using the hurley to hit it or catching by hand. The women's version of hurling is called camogie.

Horseracing

Ireland is known for breeding some of the best racehorses in the world, and a day at the races can be an exciting experience. The Curragh near Kildare is the main racing area and racecourse.

All-Ireland Final

The All-Ireland Final is the ultimate game of Gaelic football, and is held in Dublin in September. The best two teams of the year compete in the final. Thousands of fans turn the streets of Dublin into a multi-coloured celebration as they wear team colours to support their players. Kerry is the most successful team, having won 33 times since 1887. Dublin is second with 22 wins.

A hurling match is played at Croke Park stadium in Dublin.

Stay or go?

You finish your journey around Ireland in Limerick. From here it is just a short distance to Shannon airport to catch a flight home. But what if you decide to stay? What else is there to discover?

Western isles

There are several islands off the west coast of Ireland that are well worth exploring. The Aran Isles of Inishmore, Inishmaan, and Inisheer are the best known. They have ancient ruins and beautiful landscapes. Life in the Aran Islands only began to change around 100 years ago, and there are still strong Irish traditions, including the language.

Ring of Kerry

In County Kerry in southern Ireland, a road around the Iveragh Peninsula is known as the Ring of Kerry. It is 177 kilometres (110 miles) long, and includes some of the most stunning coastal scenery in Ireland. If you are feeling more adventurous, you can also explore the peninsula on foot, on the 214-kilometre (133-mile) Kerry Way.

The lakes of Donegal are some of the most picturesque in Europe, and attract thousands of visitors every year.
➤

Lakes

County Donegal and Killarney are well known for their lakes, so you could head there to enjoy some of Ireland's very best countryside. You could even take a boat trip or try a spot of fishing.

Festivals

Ireland is a land of festivals. There are religious festivals, farming festivals, art festivals, music festivals, and fishing festivals. At any time of year there is almost certainly something happening. The local tourist office will set you off in the right direction!

Tents cover a field in Fairyhouse, to the north of Dublin, where a two-day rock festival is held.

Slieve League

The north-western coasts of County Donegal are among the most dramatic in Ireland. A highlight along this stretch of coast is Slieve League. At 601 metres (1,972 feet), this is the highest sea cliff in Europe. There is a narrow path to the top if you are feeling adventurous!

Find out more

Destination Detectives can find out more about Ireland by using the books and Internet search tips listed below.

World Wide Web

If you want to find out more about Ireland, you can search the Internet using keywords such as these:

- Ireland
- Dublin
- Gaelic culture

You can also find your own keywords by using headings or words from this book. Try using a search directory such as www.google.co.uk.

The Irish Embassy

The Irish Embassy in your own country has lots of information about Ireland. You can find out about the different counties of Ireland, the best times to visit, special events such as festivals, and Irish culture. Information on Ireland can also be found at http://www.irlgov.ie, the official Government website.

Further reading

Ireland (Horrible Histories) by Terry Deary (Scholastic Ltd, 2000)

Ireland (World Tour Series) by Patrick Daley (Raintree, 2004)

Rainy Day Guide to Ireland by Orla Kearney (Gill and Macmillan, 2005)

The Story of Ireland by Stewart Ross (Orion Children's, 2001)

Timeline

3000 BC
Early farmers settle in Ireland.

600 BC
Celts arrive in Ireland.

AD 432
St Patrick arrives in Ireland and begins converting the people to Christianity.

AD 800
Beginning of Viking attacks on Ireland.

AD 916
Vikings establish a settlement at what is now Dublin.

AD 920
Vikings establish a settlement at Limerick.

1002
Brian Boru is declared King of All Ireland after defeating the Vikings.

1169
Normans from England land in Ireland, starting 800 years of war between the two countries.

1272
British conquer parts of northern Ireland.

1541
Henry VIII of England declares himself King of Ireland.

1641
Irish begin an uprising, demanding the return of lands taken from them by the British.

1845–1849
The Irish famine is caused by poor potato harvests.

1886
First Home Rule bill discussed in parliament, which would allow Ireland self-rule.

1916
Easter Rising in Dublin.

1921
Irish Free State is established.

1949
Irish Free State becomes the **Republic** of Ireland.

1951–1962
IRA campaign in North.

1955
Ireland joins the United Nations.

1985
Anglo-Irish Agreement is signed.

1990
Mary Robinson becomes the first woman president of Ireland.

1991
Ireland joins the **European Union**.

2002
The Euro becomes the official currency of Ireland.

2005
Cork is voted European Capital of Culture.

Ireland – facts & figures

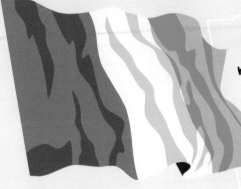

The Irish flag has three equal-sized rectangles of green, white and orange. The green represents the native people of Ireland. The orange represents the British people who settled in Ireland in the 17th century (who were supporters of a man named William of Orange). The white in the middle represents peace between these two peoples.

People and places

- Population: 4 million.
- Average life expectancy: men – 75; women – 80.
- Highest point: Carrauntoohil (1,041 metres/3,416 feet).

Money matters

- Average earnings: approx. 500 euros per week.
- Main export products: computers, chemicals, animals and animal products.
- Main import products: data-processing equipment, textiles.

Technology

- Number of land lines: 2 million.
- Number of mobile phones: 3.4 million.
- Number of computers: 1.26 million.
- Internet country code: .ie.

Glossary

AD number of years from the birth of Jesus Christ in the Christian calendar

ancestry people you are descended from

angler person who enjoys the sport of angling (fishing)

archaeology study of remains to help us understand about the past

bagpipe wind instrument in which air blown into a bag produces notes on a set of connected pipes

BC stands for "Before Christ"

bogs areas of soft, marshy land

Celts group of people who lived in much of Europe from 2000–4000 years ago

climate typical weather conditions in an area

congestion blocking of roads due to large numbers of vehicles

economy how a country makes and manages its money

European Union group of countries that help each other with trade

export selling goods to another country

float decorated platform built on a vehicle used in carnivals

forestry planting and caring for trees

Gaelic anything relating to the Celts

granite hard grey rock formed by heat beneath Earth's surface

habitat place where animals or plants live, such as a forest or the ocean

hurling Irish sport in which a leather ball is passed between players using sticks

immigrants people who move from their own country and settle in another

inlet small bay along a coastline

limestone soft rock formed by the skeletons of small animals

microchip part of a computer where all the information is decoded

organic grown without using chemicals

patron saint holy person who is the guardian of a place or people

port place where ships load and unload cargo

preserve stop from decaying or spoiling

quay platform along the edge of a port or harbour for boats to load

rebellion when a group of people try to overthrow a government or ruler

regenerate rebuild something that has worn down

republic form of government where the people rule a country

rural relating to the countryside

shamrock small plant common across Ireland

souvenir something you buy as a reminder of a hoiday

suburbs areas of housing on the outskirts of a city or town

taxes money collected by a government from income or sales

tram type of train that runs on rails through city streets

Index